Frome

IN OLD PHOTOGRAPHS

DEREK GILL

Alan Sutton Publishing Limited
Phoenix Mill · Far Thrupp · Stroud
Gloucestershire · GL5 2BU

First published 1995

British Library Cataloguing in Publication Data.
A catalogue record for this book is available from
the British Library.

ISBN 0-7509-0873-4

Typeset in 9/10 Sabon.
Typesetting and origination by
Alan Sutton Publishing Limited.
Printed in Great Britain by
Butler & Tanner, Frome, Somerset.

Contents

A view from the roof of Rook Lane church, looking east to Chapmanslade, *c.* 1950. Note the wedge of open fields of Garston Farm, a lung right into the very heart of Frome. The area is now threatened by housing developments alongside Garsdale, to the detriment of Frome as a rural town. Seen here (centre left) are the Merchants Barton factories, and the former Cockey works at Garston Road are on the right.

Introduction

In about the year 685 a group of monks wound its way along ancient trackways through the great forest which stretched from the English Channel to the Cotswolds. The monks reached a river, which they forded, and climbed uphill to a small level area in a clearing, where they stopped. Here they prepared the ground, dug foundations and built a small, stone church which they dedicated to St John the Baptist. The leader of the group went down to the riverbank, where he played his harp and sang in his clear, beautiful voice. Very soon a crowd of people gathered from small, scattered settlements, to listen to his Christian message. Many believed and were baptized in the river. This leader was St Aldhelm, Abbot of Malmesbury; gradually around his church a small community developed and thus Frome came into existence.

At first its growth was slow but by the time of the Domesday survey in 1087 Reinbald the priest held Frome (a royal manor) of the king, and it had three mills yielding 25s a year and a market which paid 46s 8d. It was still a small settlement but was certainly growing. During the later medieval period the abundance of sheep in the area resulted in the development of cloth-making. Frome prospered and expanded. From the sixteenth to the eighteenth centuries new houses were needed for the weavers and other artisans, as well as grander homes for the clothiers and dyers. Many new streets were constructed, especially in what are now known as the Trinity area and Sheppards Barton. Until the Industrial Revolution, cloth-making was a cottage industry, with the father working at his loom upstairs and the rest of the family spinning thread below. It took seven or eight spinners to keep one weaver occupied.

By the nineteenth century cloth-making was concentrated in mills, and the largest in Frome was Sheppard's mill at Spring Gardens. During the Napoleonic period Frome was renowned for its blue cloth used for army uniforms. Before 1856 dyeing used natural colourants but after that date chemicals were used. The Trinity area was originally the oad (or wode) ground where the plant which produced the blue dye was grown. Field names reflected this industry: Cut Hedges, where hedges were kept low to enable the wind to dry the dyed cloth more easily, or Rack Close, where the cloth was hung on wooden racks to dry in the sun.

After the defeat of Napoleon the cloth industry in Frome declined. As it had not kept up to date with more modern methods, it lost trade to the north of England, and its cloth was too hard wearing. By the 1830s, with empty houses and unemployment, the Poor Rate was used to sponsor emigration to Canada, where poor families could start a new life. Frome was in a bad way. Fortunately in the 1850s new industries were established, which gradually brought prosperity back to Frome. Lewis Cockey came to the town in 1680 to cast church bells, and his descendants continued the business for a hundred years, but by the nineteenth century they had turned to the gas industry. It was no accident that Frome had gas street-lighting as early as 1832. William Langford set up a small printing press in a stable of the Wheatsheaf to print labels for his medicine bottles, from which developed Butler and Tanner, now a major employer in the area. John Webb Singer, a local watchmaker, indulged his interest in metal by making church ornaments as a hobby, coinciding with a liturgical revival in the Church of England. Later three London sculptors persuaded him to build a foundry for casting statues; the figures of Boadicea on the Embankment, Justice on the Old Bailey, King Alfred at Winchester, and the lions at Capetown were all cast here. This light industrial tradition is still true today.

By good fortune Frome has retained most of its old buildings, which still reflect the prosperity brought by cloth. There are more listed buildings here than in any other town in Somerset. Modest about its potential as a place of interest, Frome still has the feel of a working town. The turning point was the saving of the Trinity area in the 1970s. Here a third of its late seventeenth-century terraced cottages had been lost ten years before. When it was proposed that the rest should be demolished, strong objections were voiced locally. The area has now been restored and is nationally renowned.

Only now is this tourist potential beginning to be realized. There was a recent suggestion that the town should claim the status of a world heritage site. Increasingly, instead of merely passing through on their way from Longleat to Bath, people are stopping to look, and are amazed at what they see.

No doubt older residents reading this book will reflect nostalgically about the Frome that has gone, but I also hope more will be strengthened in their determination to protect and enhance what remains. Frome is a town of charm, with its winding, narrow streets leading down to the Market Place. It has many nooks and crannies that constantly surprise the explorer. Socially it is also an active town, with many varied activities and events, some of which I have included here. There is no excuse to be bored in Frome.

Derek Gill
October 1994

Acknowledgements

First I wish to thank the trustees of Frome Museum for allowing me the use of photographs from their extensive collection. Many people have also lent me photographs, notably Rose Hunt, the churchwardens of Christ Church, Gerald Russell, Joe Tanner (Butler & Tanner), Robert Gill, Rodney Goodall, Ray Daniel, Alan Venn, Tony Brown (Frome Town Band), Phyl Ayles and Robert Stannard. In addition, thank you to the many people who have added to my own collection over many years. I have endeavoured to exclude any illustrations already published in Michael McGarvie's fine series of *Frome in Old Postcards*.

My task has been helped by the staff of Frome Library, and I thank them for their perseverance; and others whose memories I have tapped. Thank you, too, to Gwenn Venn who, as usual, read my script with a critical eye. I wish to record my thanks to Alan Sutton Publishing for making this book possible. Finally I am grateful to my wife, Jean, for her great help in selecting photographs, and for her suggestions and patience.

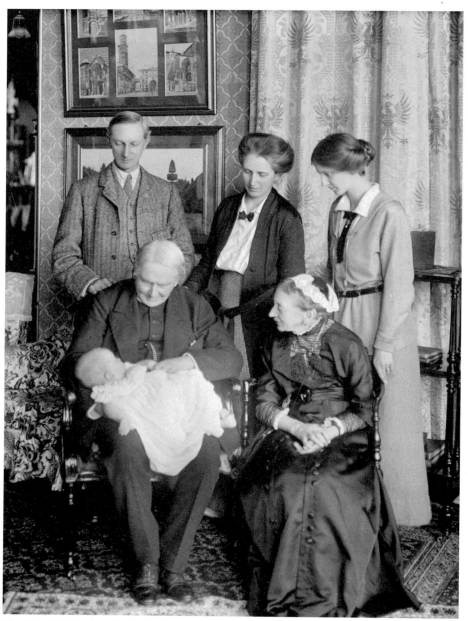

The Revd W. Arthur Duckworth and Mrs Duckworth with their great grandchild, 1916. Behind are Sir Henry and Lady Newbaldt (daughter of Mrs Duckworth) and their daughter.

SECTION ONE

School Days

Selwood School, *c.* 1895. This was a private school run by Mrs Coombs and her daughters from about 1890. At first the school was in Wine Street House; it moved to 7 South Parade in about 1902, then to South Hill in about 1910 and back to Wine Street by 1914. This charming portrait shows Mrs Coombs, surrounded by her daughters and the children. She was the wife of a Badcox grocer, Alfred Coombs, and lived at Wine Street House, where she died in 1912, aged eighty.

St John's Infants' School, 1916. The present St John's parish hall was built in 1854 as an infant school, which remained there until 1958. The mistress in this photograph is Miss Leney. One of the pupils is Carl Wilmott (second row, third from left).

Holy Trinity School, c. 1935. This was opened in 1840, two years after Holy Trinity Church, and moved to its present premises in Nunney Road in 1977. This photograph shows the mistress Mrs Bartlett and part of her class. She retired in 1944.

The flower exhibition at Christ Church Girls' School, July 1921. Mrs Morris succeeded her formidable aunt Miss Gowan as headmistress in 1917. She brought an entirely new outlook to the school and one of her innovations was this annual flower exhibition, held in the upper classroom.

Christ Church Infants' School, 1914. The photograph was taken in the playground, with the churchyard behind. The teacher on the right is probably Miss Goodbourne, known as 'Governess'; she was the mistress from 1909 to 1934.

Christ Church maypole dancers, 1930s. Back row, left to right: Poppy Staples; Jennie Hutton; Alice Bonfield; Nellie Carpenter; Doris Fortin. Front row: Florence Stokes; Ethel Bainton; Eugenie Witcombe; Florence Hunt (later Mrs Cunningham), Dorothy Greatwood (later Mrs Barnes).

Whit Monday procession, c. 1900. The tradition of giving Sunday school children a bun at Whitsun is an old one. In 1826 the boys and girls of the National School on Bath Street were 'regaled with roast beef and plum pudding by public subscription', but by 1830 they were only given pies. The Nonconformist churches also maintain this tradition and the annual Whitsun procession is still a feature of the year. The Christ Church banner is seen here on the right.

Wesley boys working in the garden, 1912. The Wesleyan Schools were established in 1863. By 1912 the teaching had become less rigid and the boys were given gardening lessons in the school garden, at the rear of the school.

Milk Street (now Vallis) School, 1898. The interior of the boys' department, on the top floor, shows the formal layout of the classroom. The different rows divided the various Standards, which were all taught in the one room. The door on the left still leads into the long corridor which runs the length of the building. The girls' school was below.

Milk Street School, c. 1923. The pupils performed *Snow White and the Seven Dwarfs* in the Palace Theatre, now the site of Brady's, at the corner of Eagle Lane and Church Steps.

Above, Class 1, Milk Street School, 1874. The girl in the back row, marked with a cross, is Mary Watts. Below are two medallions which were awarded to her for writing and geography. They are now owned by her granddaughter. Medals were distributed at the end of the Christmas term for reading, writing, arithmetic, geography, history and grammar, and were given as an incentive to maintain an improvement in the boys' and girls' departments following termly examinations. These were marked by one of the managers, who also gave out the medallions.

The Bluecoat School, *c.* 1913. It used the central part of the Blue House until 1921, and was endowed to educate poor boys. Later fee payers were introduced. In 1913 the fees were £2 2*s* a term for the 'hat boys', who wore suits as opposed to the 'foundationers' who did not. The latter were fully clothed once a year in a suit of blue cloth and supplied with shirts, bands, caps, shoes and stockings. Back row, left to right: ? Townsend; ? Cuzner; ? Barber; ? Crees; Gerald Beachem; George Gardner; ? Gould; Harry Savin; Reg Millard; Ernie Coombs. Third row: Arthur Shefford; George Dobb; Wilfred Vallis; ? Knapton; Alec Rebbick; ? Kent; Jimmy Wickendon; ? Dodge; Lou Webb; Cyril Turner; ? Sutton. Second row: John Lewis; ? Barnes; Noel Hutton; Mr S.R. Forster; Mr W. Skeet (headmaster); Mr A. Freeman; -?-; ? Rebbeck, ? Rigg. Front row: ? Champion, ? Dodge, ? York.

Keyford College, *c.* 1910. This was a private school, which moved from 8 Sunnyside to Sunny Lawn (now the site of Sunnyside Place) in 1886, where this photograph was taken. In 1906 it advertised: 'The course of instruction embraces all that is necessary to prepare boys for university examinations.' The fees were 12 guineas a term for boys under thirteen and 15 guineas for the rest, or 2 guineas for day pupils. The college closed in around 1931.

St John's College, Wallbridge, *c.* 1911.
This could be part of Wallbridge House
but cannot now be identified. The college,
established by Vicar Bennett, leased these
premises in 1893. When it closed, a
French priest, Fr Pelletant, purchased the
house in 1911 and opened his Anglo-
French School, where pupils were taught
'Greek, Latin, French and German,
Drawing and Music, Typewriting and
Shorthand'. Financial problems caused it
to close in 1913.

Selwood School, *c.* 1912. The group is photographed outside South Hill, another
building which has disappeared. It was replaced by the Memorial Hall in 1924.

Selwood School at Wine Street House, *c.* 1930. In about 1914 the school returned to Wine Street House, where it remained until its closure in 1937. These two photographs show the children in the garden at the rear of Wine Street House. At the end of the day the girls were lined up to await the call to come out separately to curtsey and say 'Good afternoon, Miss Bessie' (or whichever Miss Coombs happened to be on duty). The fees in 1919 were £1 8s a term.

Church Life

Holy Trinity bazaar, 9 August 1836. Holy Trinity Church was built in 1838 to serve the needs of the inhabitants on the western side of Frome. A bazaar was held to raise money towards its construction and this was a great success. Thomas Bunn noted in his diary: 'About half a dozen tents were placed in a beautiful field, bounded by the river. The approach was over a Chinese bridge, adorned with laurel. Two boats were in motion on the water, for such as chose an excursion on this element. The band of music was placed in a field between the river and the road, to which the populace had free access.'

St John's fête in the Market Hall, *c*. 1910. This is an interesting view of the old Market Hall, which backs on to the railway. Before the First World War an annual Forest of Trees was held in January to raise money for St John's and this may be one of those occasions.

St John's fête and bazaar, 27 June 1922. It was held on a fine summer's day in the Triangle Ground (now the Mary Baily Field) to raise £3,000 to rebuild the organ. The first terrace to be built in Somerset Road can be seen in the background. The fête was opened by Mrs Wynne Willson, wife of the new bishop of the diocese, and here the vicar, Prebendary Randolph, is presumably introducing her. In the centre are the churchwardens, G.W. Wiltshire and E.C.R. Baily.

St John's weathercock, 1923. The cock is 3 ft 4 in from bill to tail, and claw to comb, while its base is 17 in in diameter. The weathercock weighs 42 lbs in total and the cock itself 7 lb. When in position, from the top of the cock's comb to the ground is 141 ft 10 in. Here a firm of steeplejacks had been engaged to repair the spire, including regilding the weathercock.

Aldhelm Ashby outside St John's. He succeeded his grandfather as sacristan in 1903 and for forty years was a photographer and fine art dealer at 1 Bath Street, where his advertisements still adorn the walls. He died in 1958, aged sixty-six.

Christ Church Bible class, *c.* 1917. The photograph was taken in the grounds of Austin House (now Stonewall Manor), which was then the home of Major and Mrs Mallet. Back row, left to right: Donald Cross; Roger Tabor; R. Ashman; -?-*; Major Mallet; ? Hudson*; -?-*; C. White; ? Adams*. Middle row: I. Lyons; Mrs Mallet; ? Burton*. Front row: G. Bicknell, F. Elliott, ? Baker*, A. Randall; -?-; C. Groves. (* from St Aldhelm's Home, a Church of England home for waifs and strays)

Christ Church bazaar and fête, 6 June 1906. This annual event took place in the grounds of the Iron Gates. The theme that year was Elizabethan England and included a masque enacted by nearly a hundred performers. They processed from Park Road to the fête. The money raised was for the Fabric Fund.

Christ Church choir and servers, 1933. Back row, left to right: Bert Whalley; Bert Adlam; E. Minty (crucifer); Glen Lewis (behind); Charles Upward (banner-bearer); Leslie Matthews (banner-bearer). Third row: Don Cross (thurifer); James Good; Ralph Waite (churchwarden); Fr J. Howard Lewis (vicar); Reginald Dix (churchwarden); Frederick Stone; Bert Capon; Kenneth Sutton; Tom Symonds. Second row: Ralph Davis; Norman Frost; Victor Frost (organist); Fr Sheppard (curate); -?-; -?-; Joe Frost; Hugh Lewis (verger); Roland Hall; -?-; -?-. Front row -?-; -?-; -?-; Ken Miller; Robert Barnes; Bill Henley; Norman Green; -?-; Gordon Baker; -?-; -?-.

St Mary's choir and servers, c. 1912. Back row, left to right: -?-; -?-; -?-; -?-; ? Markey; -?-. Third row: -?-; -?-; ? Edgell; ? Carpenter (crucifer); R. Chivers, Alf Chivers (verger); -?-; -?-; ? Green; Tom Pike. Second row: Frank Dunford; Arthur Fricker; Herbert Sutton (organist); A. Frankum (churchwarden); Revd Glynne-Jones (vicar); Walter Cray (churchwarden); Harry Keeping (thurifer); ? Stillman; S. Newman; 'Blackie' Martin. Front row: -?-; -?-; -?-; ? Keeping; -?-; -?-.

Holy Trinity outings: before the Second World War the annual charabanc outing was a social event of parish and factory. Above, a party from Holy Trinity is off to Bournemouth, June 1920. The vicar is Revd C.R.R. Stack. Below, the choir is bound for Weymouth, 1910.

Opening Portway Methodist Church, 3 November 1910. The church replaced the United Methodist Church, which had stood on the vacant site on the bend at the bottom of Wine Street. The new church was designed by W.S. Skinner of Bath and was built by A.J. Bray of Bristol, using stone from Vallis quarries. The total cost was £898.

A bazaar held by Zion Congregational Church in the grounds of North Hill House, c. 1895. This was the home of the Le Gros family, who were staunch members of the church. The figure in the centre (with the bowler hat) was William Brett Harvey, who for many years was organist, Sunday school superintendent and deacon.

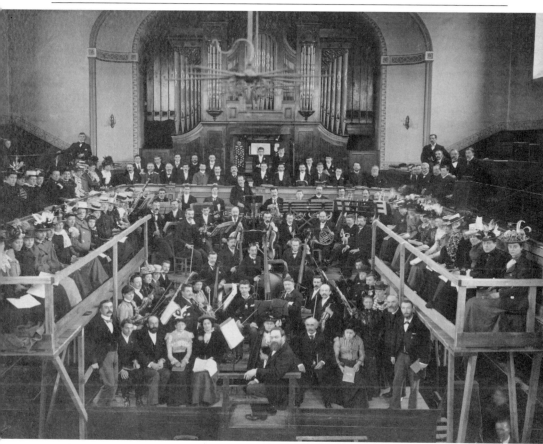

Wesley Methodist Church was, and still is, the venue for many concerts of sacred music. One of the programmes is marked 'Elijah', so perhaps the choir and orchestra are to perform Mendelssohn's masterpiece. This was the piece selected by the Free Church Choral Union in Wesley at its tenth annual festival, in February 1909. Then there were over a hundred performers, including four soloists, Mr F.C. Tucker (conductor), Roland White (organist) and Mr W.J. Harvey (president of the society).

Badcox Lane men's Bible class, 1896. Back row, left to right: ? Brimson; C. Saunders; ? Harbottle; -?-; ? Goulter; ? Harvey; -?-; ? Thrasher; ? Starr; S. Chivers. Third row: ? White; T. White; ? Bennett; ? Browning; ? Neate; ? Hurst; -?-; ? Parrot; ? Palmer; -?-; F. Coles. Second row: ? Rossiter; S Francis; ? Browning; ? Morgan; H. Palmer; ? Coombe; ? Page; -?-; ? Carpenter; ? Smith; H. Moody; -?-. Front row: ? Palmer; ? Bennett; -?-; ? White; ? White; ? Gibbs; ? Bennett; ? Palmer; ? Witcombe; ? Trollop.

Temperance Hall, *c.* 1910. This stood in Catherine Street, on the site of the present small car-park. It was opened in 1874 and cost £1,500, including the site and furniture. The building housed Frome Library from 1954 to 1964, when it was found to be unsafe and was demolished.

Rook Lane Congregational Church. The organ is still in the gallery but was moved down to the body of the chapel in 1929. On the right of the pulpit is a memorial to the first four pastors. The church closed in 1968, following the amalgamation with Zion (now Frome United Reformed Church) and for twenty-five years the building stood neglected and crumbling. Now it has been restored.

SECTION THREE

People at Work

Wallbridge Mills, *c.* 1920. Tucker's was the last cloth mill in Frome and a tradition of centuries ended when it closed in 1965. The firm was founded by Alfred Tucker of Trowbridge, who bought the premises in 1868 for his son to produce West of England cloth. This is the carding room and the end of the tape condenser.

Wallbridge Mills *c.* 1920. Above, the menders, inkers and spilers at work in the mill. Below, the range of buildings beside the river, seen from the railway, with the footpath from Willow Vale crossing the field. The large mill building in front of the chimney was destroyed by fire some thirty years ago. Above the name board are the roof tops of the Garston Road area.

Chiffon hands, *c.* 1900. Thompson & Le Gros operated the mill at Merchants Barton from about 1840 until 1926, manufacturing silk and crape fabrics, crêpe de Chine and gloves. At its peak it employed some four hundred hands, mainly young women and girls. In 1926 the premises were purchased by Messrs J.H. Nott from Swansea.

Employees of Messrs J.W. Singer & Sons Ltd, *c.* 1918. During the First World War, while the men were in the forces, Singer's was forced to employ women, which inevitably brought a change in social attitudes. During this time the firm was requisitioned by the government to make munitions.

Singer's architectural moulders, 27 September 1913. Back row, left to right: Charlie Perkins; Jim Dowden. Third row: Len Stockting; Tom Brimson; Arthur Edgell; Harold Rodgers; Godfrey Beauchamp; Jim Moody. Second row: Herbert Hagley; Bill Burchell; Jack Gifford; Charlie Axford; Bert Pope. Front row: 'Topsy' Coleman. The photograph was taken and presented to Bill Burchell when he left for Canada. Gifford and Stockting were also statuary moulders; the former made part of Boadicea, and the latter was engaged on the fountains in Trafalgar Square, the bronze doors of the Bank of England and the Haig memorial.

Singer's laboratory, c. 1920. This is a print from one of many glass negatives rescued from the factory. The figures on the shelves are plaster moulds awaiting casting. The man may be C.W. Patch, cashier and later company secretary.

This dragon is being prepared for Cardiff City Hall, 1904. It was made by Singer's in lead from models by Mr H.C. Fehr, and was constructed to an unusually large scale in this material. Cast in seven pieces, it was built up in an iron frame and burnt together in position on the dome over the City Hall council chamber.

St John's corona, before 1890. It was made by John W. Singer in 1854 and hung under the chancel arch, but was removed in 1892 when the rood screen was erected. The present roof structure exactly matches that in the photograph. The chancel gates and Lady Chapel screen are also Singer's work, as is the church plate.

At Butler & Tanner (as are the following three photographs): a letterpress two-revolution machine in the Selwood Road factory, *c.* 1901. The machine printed on one side of the paper, thirty-two pages at a time. Note the operator's high collar and cravat.

The Dreadnought was the third machine to be installed in the Adderwell factory in 1910. A letterpress book rotary fed from a reel, which it sheeted, printed on both sides and folded to size – 192 pages on each revolution. Mr Nutley is in charge.

A 1926 letterpress perfector from America. This allowed fully automatic printing on both sides of the sheets, up to 128 pages per revolution. The book being printed is Ward-Lock's *Wonder Book of Aircraft* and Messrs Horler and Turner are in charge. Ties were still *de rigueur.*

The first automatic hard-back binding line in Europe, made by arranging a series of free-standing 1935 American machines so that each fed the next. The bookbinders in charge are Fred Foster and Jack Bartlett.

Post Office staff, 1912. The post office was at 6 Bath Street from 1864 until it moved to the Market Place in 1914. Back row, left to right: Luke Lapham; George Bennett; Arthur Carver; Joshua Keen; Harry Lyons; Herbert Newport; William Smith; W. Harding; Charles Coles; Frederick Windsor; Tom Smith; John Horler. Third row: Percy Edwards; Edgar Crespin; Harry Speed; Arthur Wall; Frank Harrison; William Treasure; George Edwards; William Harbottle; Charles Nutt; Arthur Harding; William Green. Second row: George Williams; Harry Pike; S. Palmer (assistant postmaster); H. Chorley; W. White (postmaster); Frank Webber; Godfrey Jacobs; W. Harvey; Robert Foster. Front row: Ben Mould; Will Button; Will Skeplorn; Fred Stocker.

A messenger boy, 1945. On leaving school, boys could be employed for three years by the Post Office as messenger boys. There were three in Frome and their job was to deliver telegrams. They were provided with a uniform and a bicycle, which they were required to maintain. The telegram was carried in a pouch fixed to the belt. The salary at the end of the last war was 14s 6d a week with an extra 1s 6d for two hours' work on Sundays. Journey times were specified and boys were expected to keep to them. Telegrams were abolished in 1982. The photograph shows M. Poole, then aged fifteen.

Seward's builder's yard, Butts Hill, *c*. 1900. Fifth from the left (with the boater) is Osman Seward, son of the founder of the firm, which started in around 1873. By 1900 there were thirty-six employees – journeymen, labourers and apprentices – with a total weekly wages bill of £50. Much of Butts Hill, Somerset Road and elsewhere was built by the firm. The premises are now used by Sharpe & Fisher.

The introduction of electricity to Frome, *c*. 1903. The Edmundson's Electricity Corporation built the station behind Palmer Street in 1903 for £20,156, and managed it for the UDC. A supply to consumers began on 1 July 1904. Here the cable is being laid along Portway, towards the junction with Vicarage Street, and the work is being supervised by Mr W.C.B. Hillman. The wall belongs to the Portway Hotel.

EASTMEAD & BIGGS,

Telegrams—"BIGGS, FROME."

FROME, SOMERSET.

£225

NO Chains.
NO Belts.
NO Battery.
NO Vibration.
NO Trouble.

£225

Silent Drive.
High Efficiency.
Ball Bearings.
Three Speeds.
Geared Steering.

The EASTMEAD-BIGGS VOITURETTE,

$3\frac{1}{2}$ H.P., Water Cooled, Natural Circulation, MAGNETO-ELECTRIC IGNITION, Two Seats, 3in. Pneumatic Tyres, Basket with ample luggage room, Interchangeable Parts, Fully Guaranteed. Highest-class British Work throughout.

The voiturette was designed and made in Frome by Mr T.J. Biggs, between 1901 and 1904. It was financed by Mr F. Eastmead, a London lift manufacturer, and though technically advanced it was underfunded and poorly marketed. The company closed and the plant and equipment were sold in October 1904. Mr Biggs, a draughtsman of Raleigh cycles, became chief engineer to Humber, designing cycle parts and Grand Prix cars.

The Achilles, *c.* 1904. This was also made in Frome, by B. Thompson & Co. Ltd, and was registered in 1901 with a capital of £3,000. The car was advertised for 'the man of moderate means' and priced between £145 and £300. One is known to exist still. Had these two manufacturers succeeded, Frome might have rivalled Coventry!

A Visit to a Modern Tyre Factory.

The St. John's Rubber Mills, Frome
Owned by Messrs. Wallington, Weston & Co.

Mr. Albert Wallington.

Mr. William George Weston.

Wallington & Weston moved to Frome from Limpley Stoke in 1896 and manufactured india rubber at St John's Mills, Adderwell. In 1946 the firm moved to Vallis Way and the Adderwell premises were taken over by William Pinchin & Co. Ltd, which made paint. Now Cuprinol occupies the site. Pictured are the founders, Albert Wallington and William Weston.

At E.C. Cockey & Sons Ltd, *c.* 1925. Lewis Cockey first cast church bells in about 1680 in Milk Street. The business was continued by his descendants, and in the nineteenth century the firm began making items for the gas industry, including this gasometer under construction at their Garston works. Gas standards, bollards and railings are still reminders of the firm. Here, to the right of the foundry, is Garston Farm roof, with the railway beyond.

10 Vallis Way, *c.* 1890. On the right are the offices, including paint and colour departments, of William Coombs, with a showroom above for gas fittings, window glass, pipes, etc. Coombs lived in the house on the left, which now has a small central first-floor window and dormers. The top of the iron porch, which has recently been removed, can be seen here above the shrubbery. In between is a warehouse and stores. The little boy on the extreme left is Edgar Bush. William Coombs died in 1899, aged forty-nine, and was succeeded by his son Herbert. The Vallis Way/Broadway link now crosses the site.

SECTION FOUR
People

A group of ladies outside Catherine Hill House, home of the photographer, John Bell, *c.* 1900. The proximity to Badcox Lane Baptist Church suggests that the group formed part of the congregation.

The Rawlings family, *c*. 1887. Samuel Tovey Rawlings and his family lived at Oriel Lodge, Christchurch Street, next to his carding works. At the time of this portrait, by Frome photographer W.A. Brookes, Samuel was forty-five and his wife Emily forty-eight. Their surviving five daughters, shown here, are probably, from the left: Marion (aged twelve); Lucy (nineteen); Ada (twenty-one); Emily (twenty-two); Rose (thirteen).

Photographers at Egford, *c*. 1895. They are gathered outside the 'haunted' house, off the lane leading uphill from the cattle grid at Egford to Great Elm. The house is now a heap of rubble. The photograph was taken by Mr Vallis.

Frederick Charles Bray, 1902. He was a son of Charles Axford Bray, founder of the printing and stationery business in Church Street (see page 82), and this photograph shows him after his return from the Boer War. He later emigrated to Guernsey, Canada.

Mrs Emily Harrold and her husband Frederick were very involved in the musical life of Frome, especially St John's Church. She was organist there from 1877 until 1915, at the same time as her husband was choirmaster, and is shown seated at the organ. Frederick was a chemist at 4 Bath Street.

These two photographs, dating from around 1913, are interesting in showing two modes of travelling of the period. Here two ladies prepare for a cycle ride from the photographer's studio in Keyford. One, or both, is a member of the Weaver family.

For many years Herbert Weaver was a plumber, decorator, glazier and paperhanger at 2 Palmer Street. In this photograph his wife Winifred and baby son Graham exercise in the park.

Seven children from the Gay family of Frome, *c*. 1895. The boy on the right (in the straw hat) is Jesse Gay. It is a charming group, and shows the style of dresss typical of the period.

Ethel Gay, 1918. Ethel was one of the first to join the WAAF (Women's Auxiliary Air Force) during the First World War. Afterwards she met and married Frank Maher, an Australian soldier.

Mr George William Hodder at Badcox. The red-brick Badcox Parade was built by John Hodder in 1890 and his sixth son, George, opened the pharmacy in the corner premises. He maintained this until his death in 1929. Described as a modest, quiet man he nevertheless served as chairman of the Chamber of Commerce, as secretary of the YMCA and as a deacon at Badcox Lane Baptist Church. The pharmacy still exists.

Mr Dyke and his trap, *c.* 1912. Frank Henry Dyke succeeded to his father's Fancy Bazaar in Catherine Street, and was a prolific photographer, printing many postcards and albums of local views. He seems not to have a care in the world, but perhaps that is deceptive for he committed suicide in February 1925, aged only forty-six.

An Edwardian wedding, *c.* 1903. These charming photographs were found in the loft of 70 Nunney Road and one has 'Mr Davis, Broadway' pencilled on the back. These two clues suggest that it was the wedding of Walter Henry and Emily Davis. They lived at Brierley, Broadway, when their daughter Evelyn was born in 1904, and then at Hartgells, 70 Nunney Road. The elderly couple above are probably the bridegroom's grandparents, and the Edwardian chair may be a wedding present. Walter Davis was an engineer.

Selwood Cottage (now Lodge) is shown with its original thatched roof, c. 1884. At that time it was the home of Thomas Byard Sheppard, who poses with his dog. His daughter Susan stands in the doorway. It was the fashion for friends to meet at the house for breakfast and Thomas Bunn recounted walking there early for a gathering of friends and relations.

The grotto in the garden of Selwood Cottage. Back row, left to right: Edith Mico Sheppard; Augusta Sheppard (d. 1890); Thomas Byard Sheppard (d. 1888); their daughter Mary Ann; Alfred; Thomas B.W. Sheppard; Annie; -?-; -?-. Front row: Edward Sheppard; Janet; Amy B. Sheppard; N. Biddle; Aunt Agnes.

SECTION FIVE
Events

Queen Victoria's diamond jubilee procession, 1897. National events were celebrated in Frome by processions through the streets, parties and children's sports. Here, the procession wends its way along the traditional route of Christchurch Street West. In the foreground is Frome Fire Brigade, headed by a cart which carries Captain Rawlings and two fireman. It is followed by the two engines (steamer and manual).

The Prince and Princess of Wales (the future George V and Queen Mary) at Longleat House before the re-opening and consecration of Glastonbury Abbey, 22 June 1909. Included in the group are Randall Davidson (Archbishop of Canterbury), the 5th Marquess of Bath (to the right), the Marchioness of Bath (seated second from right) and, seated on the ground, their children Lady Mary Thynne and Lord Henry Frederick Thynne (future 6th Marquess of Bath, who died in 1992).

The Prince and Princess of Wales in Bath Street, 1909. Frome has never had an official royal visit, but members of the Royal Family have passed through, as here when they drove through from Longleat to Laverton and Midsomer Norton without stopping, to the disappointment of those lining the streets. Christ Church School logbook records that the 'royal party was enclosed in motorcars, and very few children recognised them'. The princess was 'seated in the carriage nearest the children and responded to their welcome by waving her hand and bowing and smiling'.

The funeral procession for Samuel Tovey Rawlings, September 1912. He was captain of Frome Fire Brigade from 1887 to 1903 and made it a much more professional body. His funeral procession from Oriel Cottage to the Vallis Road cemetery was headed by fire brigade members. Following were a hand bier laden with flowers, the coffin on an open funeral car, coaches containing family mourners, and workpeople from the South Parade works. Along the route blinds were drawn as a mark of respect.

Lady Bath starting the new engine, 23 February 1895. Frome Fire Brigade had organized a Japanese bazaar in the Market Hall to raise money for a steam Shand Mason engine. The theme caught the imagination of the public and £794 was raised, more than enough to buy the engine. The new one could throw 360 gallons of water a minute to a height of 140 ft. The machine proudly featured on brigade letter-headings for many years. Here, Lady Bath is turning the little wheel to turn on the steam, while Captain Rawlings (in the helmet) stands proudly to the right. Lady Bath also made a speech.

Egford Reservoir under construction, 1879. The need for a public water supply had been discussed since 1870, and the Frome water works was finally opened on 22 March 1880, without ceremony. The first house laid on was Garston Lodge and 433 premises were connected by 1887.

Tank in the park: this First World War tank was presented to Frome by the Army Council to commemorate the 'important part played by the Frome War Savings Committee to the country's war effort'. It was unveiled in December 1919 and remained until the outbreak of the Second World War, when it went the way of many railings and ironwork, and was melted down for armaments.

The general election declaration of December 1910. This building in Christchurch Street West was Frome's police station until 1954. The results of the election for the Frome Division were: Sir John Barlow (Liberal), 5,944; Mr C.T. Foxcroft (Conservative), 5,366; the Liberal majority was 578 votes.

Frome Liberal Party Headquarters at 21 Christchurch Street West are 'decorated' for the general election of 23 January 1906. The premises are now a newsagency. The result of the poll is in the window to the right of the 'cheap food' notice: John Emmott Barlow (Liberal), 6,297; Charles T. Foxcroft (Conservative) 4,552; the Liberal majority was 1,745. Mr Barlow later addressed the crowd from here and from the George Hotel. He was MP for Frome from 1892 to 1895 and 1896 to 1918, and was succeeded by Sir Percy Hurd, grandfather of Douglas.

A Labour demonstration to celebrate the formation of a Trade and Labour Council for Frome, 16 September 1917. The participants mustered at Wallbridge and paraded through the town to the Co-operative field in Nunney Road. They were headed by the town band and two banners. The Council consisted of seven societies, with a membership of over a thousand.

The General Strike from 4 to 12 May 1926 had a mixed effect on Frome. The railway and printing works were badly hit, but not Singer's. The unions involved were the Typographical Association, the National Union of Bookbinders, Machine Rulers and Paper Workers, and the railway unions such as ASLEF, whose strike committee is shown here.

Damage to the portico of the George Hotel, 23 October 1918. Mr Wilfred Hasell from Wanstrow had driven to Frome on market day at 12.20, and after dropping off his wife and young child, drove his spring float to the George for a delivery. While there, a lorry belonging to the Bristol Tramways Co. from Bath, heavily laden with several tons of metal for Singer's, skidded at the bottom of Bath Street and collided with the George. The sill and mullions of the commercial room window were shattered, along with the lower pillar of the portico. Falling masonry fatally wounded Mr Hasell on the head. The portico was immediately shored up and was demolished that afternoon.

Floods in Willow Vale, pictured at 11 am on 10 February 1923. Heavy overnight rain had caused the usual flooding of the roads at Feltham, Blatchbridge, Wallbridge and Willow Vale, where it was a foot deep. On this occasion the Blue Boar had over 3 ft of water inside. The Market Place frequently flooded after severe storms; the last time was in 1978, when a rowing boat had to ferry people from one side to the other.

A fire at Wallbridge Flour Mills, 13 April 1908. It broke out in the early morning and within two hours the buildings had been gutted, causing several thousand pounds' worth of damage. The fire was described as the 'biggest for years'. There was a long delay before the steamer arrived, because the employees of the livery stables in Willow Vale did not hear the alarm, so the horses could not be fetched to pull the steam engine to the scene.

The Great Fire of Cheap Street, 4 August 1923. The most serious fire to hit Frome for many years, it destroyed nos 9, 10 and 17 in the street. The fire brigade had only just returned from fighting a farm fire at Laverton when it was called here. If it had not arrived when it did, much more of Cheap Street would have been lost, including the adjoining timber-framed no. 11. The stonework of the present Settle Restaurant still shows the pinking caused by the heat of the blaze.

Jesse Gay and a carnival elephant, *c.* 1920. Small, individual entries have always been a feature of the carnival and here is one. Jesse Gay is in the top hat.

The Katchem Quick Kops and their adapted Austin 7 were a regular and amusing feature of Frome carnivals, from the 1960s to 1980s, with their crazy humour and daring antics. In 1963 the Kops appeared on the stage of the Gaumont Cinema to coincide with a film *On the Beat*, featuring Norman Wisdom. They took out the sparking plugs and ran on the battery. In the foyer of the cinema, from left to right: Stuart Randall; Michael Coleman; Cedric Williams (above); Pat Hollerhead; Keith Hart; Ray Daniel; Peter Chapman; Adam Tredgett; -?-; Derek Prosser; Jonathan Ionides (under the car).

SECTION SIX

Working and Playing Together

Coronation celebrations, 12 May, 1937. National events have always been celebrated with enthusiasm locally, and on this occasion there was a procession through the town, a programme of sports, and a tea for the children. The entertainment in the evening included a boxing display and fireworks, as with the celebrations of George V's jubilee in 1935. Here, the fire brigade, which took part in the procession with its engine, parades outside the fire station under Chief Officer H. Newport.

Frome Town AFC, 1912/13. The club had been established on 7 June 1904. The photograph includes C. Axford; H. Browning; D. Cottle; E. Burden; W. Wright; W. Earle; W. Burchell; W. Mills; J. Clift (secretary); S. Seale; A. Dudden; S. Richardson; G. Horler; H. Topp; H. Burgess; J. Wilcox; G. Davis; L. Wheeler; L. Edwards; W. Shackleton; R. Moody and C. Harris.

Milk Street Council School Old Boys AFC, 1931/32. The team champions of the Frome League and the Trowbridge League Division One. Back row, left to right: Mr Smart; Alec White; Bert Peters; Cyril Burt (linesman); Austin Pearce; Mr Carpenter. Centre row: Reg Rodgers; Spence Coles; Arthur Sheppard; Fred Benger; Ken Bull; Ron Carpenter; Gerald Carpenter; Jack Carpenter. Front row: W. Smart; Ron Coles; Herbert Larcombe; Sydney Burt; S. Ruddick; Herbert Sweet; Bill Harris.

Frome Swimming Club water polo team, 1909. Before the opening of the Victoria Baths in 1899, annual aquatic sports were held in the river, by a field near the railway station. The team shown here won the 1909 Dorset & District League. Back row, left to right: T. Davey; W.G. Dance (treasurer); T. Croad; Dr Dalby (president); C.I. Young (secretary). Centre row: H. Wilton; E.D. Perry (vice-captain); A. Wheeler (captain); J. Deacon; C. Dennis. Front row: H. Palmer; A. Young; C. Young.

Frome water polo team in the old Victoria Baths, 1935. Back row, left to right: Tom Croad (?); Arthur Wheeler; Freddie Stone; Ken Farrant; -?-; -?-; Jack Berry; Harry Lee. Centre row: Owen Batten; John Wheeler; -?-; -?-. Front row: Ken Russell; Bernard Wheeler; Don Lewis. At that time the chairman of the FUDC did not wear a chain, so the man in the centre may have been the chairman of the Western Counties Swimming Association.

Bowling, *c.* 1890. Before the present green at Butts Hill was opened in 1915, bowls was played at Southill, the site of the Memorial Hall, where these photographs were taken. Above, a corner of Rook Lane Chapel can be seen on the right and the top cottages of Bath Street on the left. In the centre is part of the roof of the Lamb Brewery.

Red Triangle Cricket Club, 1920. The Red Triangle hut was built in 1920 for the Frome Victory Club, to provide for the social welfare, recreation, self-improvement and enjoyment of men, women and girls over sixteen. Tennis, cricket and football clubs were immediately formed. Back row, left to right: H.G. Parker; A. Northeast; W. Barrett (secretary); E. Pope; J. Wickenden; R.W. Slowcombe; G.E. Taylor. Front row: A. Badder (scorer); H.W. Pope, Revd E.G. Mortimer (captain); A.P. Ames (president); G.S. Hodder (vice-captain); C. Earle. Inset: J.P. Parker; J.T. Croad (treasurer); E. Smith.

The 24th Frome Oddfellow's flower show committee, August 1907. The show was held in a field at Portway near the station. It included a fun fair and the finale was a fireworks display. Back row, left to right: W. Adlam; W. Nash; E.J. Noble; A. Vincent; P.B. Rigg; A. Lyons; H. Carpenter; A. Cray; J. Perry; H.F. Barber. Third row: E.M. Mutlow*; H. Gandy*; T. Bishop; J. Bellinger; C.A. Bray; R.P. Coombs; S. Elliott; G. Thick; H.J. Watson; H.W. Minty. Second row: T.H. Woodland; W. Hutchings; E. Vallis; W.C. Young*; W. Carpenter*; T. Challis*; H.E. Ames (chairman); F.C. Dance (vice-chairman); F.C. Rendell (secretary); J. Ace Beynon (treasurer); E.F. Bishop. Front row: J.W. Brewer*; C. Baily; A. Elton; T. Coles; W.H. Tapp*. (*judges)

The Home Guard, 1945. The Local Defence Volunteers was formed by the government in May 1940 and was renamed the Home Guard two months later. It was for men aged seventeen to sixty-five who were not called up, and disbanded on 31 December 1945. The group seen here includes Maj. Ronald Vallis (back row, far left), RSM Glover (back row, third from right), and (front row, from left) Sgt. Eric Lewis, Mrs Vallis and Herbert Scott (chairman of FUDC).

The Frome Company marches along Christchurch Street West, headed by Maj. Vallis, its commanding officer.

Frome Fire Brigade celebrating the wedding of the Duke of York (later George V), 6 July 1893. The brigade demonstrated the new engine in the Market Place with water jets lit by lime lights and coloured fires. Pictured outside the Public Offices, Capt. S.T. Rawlings stands on the engine, nearest the horse. On the engine, in the back row are 1st Lt. T.B.W. Sheppard (fourth from left), Eng. E.A. Coombs and on the right Capt. Rawlings, with 2nd Lt. H.T. Rawlings just showing in the next row.

The 25th Division, Royal Field Artillery, on parade in a deserted Market Place early one Sunday morning, 1916. The men are ready to march to St John's for church parade led by Band Leader W.H. Stokes.

Frome Town Military Band, 1911. The conductor is Mr W.H. Stokes (with the baton), and the secretary is Mr F. Milton Russ (in a suit).

The band in front of the new park bandstand, 1924. Mr Stokes is on the right in the bowler hat and gloves. On Thursdays from May to the end of September, the bandstand was used for dancing. Mr Stokes declined to conduct and the band was supervised by the bandmaster Mr H. Davidge. It was the 'in thing' to stroll around the park to meet one's acquaintances.

Frome Board of Guardians of the Frome Union outside its offices in Christchurch Street West, *c.* 1930. This was established in 1836 and was responsible for building the workhouse and providing Poor Relief. Gradually, other bodies took over its powers, especially the Urban and Rural Councils. It was eventually abolished in 1930. This photograph includes (front row) Mrs Lanfear Tanner, Mr E. Tylee (vice-chairman), Revd R.W. Baker (chairman), Mr Edgar R. Singer (vice-chairman) and Miss Mary Baily.

The last photograph of Frome UDC before its abolition in 1974. It is pictured in the Council Chamber at North Hill House. Standing left to right: Peter Bardgett; Jim Eames; George Coleman; Mrs Janet Turner; Norman Maggs; Arthur Evemy; Cliff Lewis (engineer and surveyor); Donald Crouch (finance officer); Reginald Jones; James Compton (housing officer); Mrs Eileen Edmonds; Herbert Scott; Rodney Goodall; Dr Noel Newman (Medical Officer of Health); Sidney Underwood; Frederick Traylen. Seated: Tom Towndrow (clerk); Peter Belham (chairman); Mrs Gillian Balchin; Kenneth Miller (vice-chairman).

Frome & District Operatic Society. In about 1900 the Magpies concert party was formed, which became the operatic society in 1906; its first production was *Trial by Jury*. All the early productions were held in the old Market Hall, until the opening of the Memorial Hall in 1925. The photograph above may be of *Merrie England*, first performed by the society in 1914. Below, more certainly, is the cast of *The Pirates of Penzance* in 1929. Percy Oswick played Maj.-Gen Stanley and Sydney Stockting the policeman. Also seen here is Marion Carrodus (front left).

Frome Drama Club, 1955. The Fromefield Players, formed in 1945 as a play-reading group, soon became the Frome Drama Club. Above, a scene from Shaw's *Pygmalion* (December 1955). Standing, left to right: Hilary Daniel; Vera Oswick; Rosabelle Weeks; Margaret Court; Angela Maitland; Jack Hornsey; Kaila Mathison; John Phillips. Seated: Harry Driscoll; Hugh Stanley (producer); Noreen Witcombe. Below, a scene from *And so to bed* (April 1955), a play set at the time of Samuel Pepys. The cast, from left to right: Vera Oswick; Horace Thicke; Keith Pearce; Noreen Witcombe; Alan Venn; Arthur Court; Angela Maitland; Michael Upsall.

Christ Church 3rd Frome Scouts, February 1926. The troop was re-formed in 1924 by the curate, Revd R.H. Edwards. He is seen here on the left, with his successor, Charles Upward, on the right. The scouts met on Thursdays in a large room at the back of 18 Butts Hill. The parish magazine recorded that it was 'impossible to run a troop without strict discipline and this will be enforced in the future'. The first camp was held in Charlton House Park, near Kilmersdon, in August 1926. The aeroplane pictured was available for short flights.

St John's 4th Frome Guides, c. 1932. They are seen outside their room in a building on the site of the present St John's School hall, facing Christchurch Street East. Miss Ruth Polehampton, captain and District Commissioner, stands behind the left-hand cup. In the same row (from the left) are Kate Burns (flag bearer), Eunice Overend and Winnie Young, and, on the other side of Miss Polehampton, are Kathy King (wearing glasses) and Daphne Lapham. In the front row are Iris Walwin (second from left), Dorothy James, Katherine Wingrove and ? Sutton (second from right). In front of the unleaded window is ? Morgan.

Open Spaces

Frome from Willow Vale, *c.* 1830. This stylized etching shows the division of the river, with the mill stream to the right, now its real course. On the extreme right, the Willow Vale Queen Anne Terrace is visible, before the addition of the riverside front gardens. The gate pillars of no. 15, with their round stone tops, can also been seen. St John's Church is clearly visible, with Wesley, Christ Church and Sheppard's Barton further along the skyline.

Selwood Hospital. The old workhouse was built in 1837; this later became Weymouth Hospital and finally Selwood Hospital, before its recent closure. Its grounds were always beautifully maintained, as these two photographs illustrate. The view above shows part of the drive, and below is the front entrance. The hospital and grounds have now been developed by a housing association.

The Victoria Park, *c.* 1910. It was opened in 1897 to commemorate the diamond jubilee of Queen Victoria. Above, the slower pace of life at that time is reflected by the method of mowing the grass. Below is the site of the present bowling green and the entrance from Park Road.

The Leaze. This avenue of trees is now just a memory but it once marked the carriageway from Frome to Vallis Manor, the home of the Leversedge family for three hundred years. There is still a footpath here, leading from Vallis Road across fields to the remains of the great hall. This is the highest point of Frome, with extensive views across Wiltshire.

Vallis Vale bridge, 1907. A local beauty spot, the vale has always been an area for local recreation. Many locals learned to swim in the river before the Victoria Baths were built, and downstream of the cradle bridge was a rifle range. From the 1890s until the last war the Soberest Quarry Company operated here, and the line of the tramway which carried the stone from their small quarry faces to Hapsford can still be traced. The quarry faces have now returned to nature and several limestone kilns also survive.

Vallis Vale rock face, 1910. The geological unconformity at Vallis is internationally renowned and has made it a Site of Special Scientific Interest. The inferior oolite rests directly on the carboniferous limestone, with millions of years of rock formation missing. The tramlines carried rock from the small quarries to Hapsford on trucks pulled by two small engines, the Robin and the Wren.

Vallis Vale cradle bridge, *c.* 1900. This bridge has now been replaced by a metal one on the same foundations and spans the Mells river just below its confluence with the Egford Brook. Tramlines crossed the river just upstream but only the foundations are now visible. The photographer's wife, Mrs Vallis, seen here in Edwardian dress, surveys the scene.

Bedlam mill, *c.* 1900. There are still traces of this former woollen mill, including the walls of the sluice gate, although the wheel has gone. It lies beside the footpath through Vallis to Great Elm.

At Adderwell, Frome

Adderwell Lane. This path leads from Adderwell towards Feltham but is now very overgrown. The back of The Mount development is now on the right, while the ground on the left slopes very steeply down to the river.

Adderwell, Frome
Photo F. H. Dyke

Adderwell from the site of Southfields, *c.* 1904. On the horizon (left) is Frome station while off the photograph, to the right of the bridge, is Southfield Farm. The premises of Cuprinol and Butler & Tanner now extend almost to the river on the left, making the view difficult to identify. Perhaps the two buildings above the train are the former Rodden Rectory, now Riverside, and Easthill, now demolished.

Clink, 1912. These two scenes of rural beauty are now impossible to identify. There has been a rapid development of housing on the north-eastern side of Frome over the last twenty years and a country lane is now a town road. The view below, labelled 'Badger's Hill', is not recognizable, even with the house on the left, and there is nothing distinctive in the view above.

The Changing Streetscape

Market Place, *c.* 1907. This lively scene dates from before the Post Office move to the Market Place in 1914 and before motor cars. Boots the Chemist was then an ironmonger's, probably run by Mr Penny, and it advertises Humber cycles. Halfords is now on the site of Charles Waters, wine and spirit merchant, whose advertisement on the roof reads 'W. & A. Gilbey's Wines & Spirits'. Are they sacks of coal in the centre, and what is the man with the baskets selling?

Cheap Street, 1870. This is a very accurate drawing by S.J. Speller and although most of the shop fronts have been replaced, little has altered above, except Vincent's on the right (no. 20), where the frontage has now been completely rebuilt. It may be Thomas Baily Vincent, a clothier, hatter and hosier, standing in the doorway. Frederick Pickford, whose doorway is on the extreme right, was here from around 1860 to around 1880. On the left, Mr Morgan, with the oval hanging sign (no. 6), was the shoemaker here from about 1870 while William Wells (no. 4) was a furniture dealer and cabinet maker. Note the hooks over the shop window.

Cheap Street, c. 1890. The spire of St John's is visible above the Albion Inn, now The Settle, whose bay window is now long gone. To its right, Bellamy's Leather Warehouse traded from around 1880 to 1894, but its bow window is now gone. Alfred Vincent's fishmonger's, above the Albion, had stone tiles. On the left, Simeon Bailey's Bristol Drapery Mart traded in the building until it was destroyed by the Cheap Street fire of 1923. Up the hill, Mr Harvey was a tinman and ironmonger in a building which dates from around 1500 and which is now occupied by AMICA.

Cheap Street, 1913. The 'Rand Crisis' poster outside Holloway's newsagency (which closed in 1993) dates the postcard. On the left, Mr Whittaker's tobacconist's at no. 2 traded from 1905 to 1958, and the Singer sewing-machine shop (no. 23) was in this street from 1898. Shop fronts are altered with changing fashions, not always to the benefit of the street scene.

A butcher's cart, *c.* 1898. The shop at the top of Cheap Street was a butcher's shop from 1830 to 1923, when Simeon Bailey moved here following the loss of his premises in the fire. It had been Stubbs & Sons' from 1893 to 1923. The shop front glazing bars have now been replaced but upstairs has not changed. To the left, no. 13 (now Melinda Travel) was rebuilt in 1931, using many original materials. At the premises beyond the ladder, F.G. Legg was a picture-frame maker from 1896 to 1900.

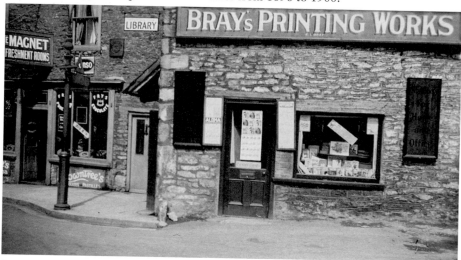

Bray's Printing Works. This is the front of Marchant's House (see page 112), which was destroyed in an act of vandalism by the Urban Council to construct Saxonvale. To the left is Church Street, towards the present fish and chip shop. The doorway to the printing works was around the left-hand corner of the building, beneath the library hanging sign.

King Street, 1922. The George Hotel is clearly recognizable at the end of the street. The hairdresser Boddington's is now Pang's Fish Bar, while the building on the left is the Halifax Estate Agency, then Harding's. Interestingly the Midland Bank is being built, which dates the photograph.

The Waggon & Horses, Gentle Street. The 'Froome Flying Wagon', a fast stagecoach, used to start from the courtyard at the rear of this seventeenth-century inn, and in the eighteenth century it took two days to reach London. In the late 1950s the inn was converted into flats.

A view from the electricity tower, 1905. This contact print was taken from the scaffolding when the electricity works chimney was built. The chimney was reduced in 1964 and later demolished. The Lamb Brewery buildings are on the left, and the roof of the National School is in front. Note the many trees in Frome.

A view from the roof of Rook Lane Church, c. 1950. Notice the trees on North Hill. The chimney belongs to the electricity works at Rook Lane, the Literary Institute is above and the Blue House is on the right. North End is visible to the left, while the land beyond is now mostly developed for housing.

Bath Street, 1907. The railings disappeared at the beginning of the last war and so has the creeper on the building, which is now the St John Ambulance Hall but was then Mr Percy Wheeler's Auction Mart. The tall building behind the cottages was part of Cockey's foundry and has now gone, too. On the right, many of the trees have been replaced by the concrete rockery of the Royal British Legion's frontage.

Bath Street, 1907. The bay window of the Wheatsheaf has gone and its porch replaced. Jackson's building still exists but the shop front has been altered and it is now Bolloms. The corner shop on the left was owned for a short time by John Gradidge in addition to his larger premises opposite. The boys would not dare stand in the road now.

Bath Street, *c.* 1887. Taken at the same time as the photograph below, this view shows the corner of Frederick Snook's China and Glass Warehouse, which re-opened as the Lamb Commercial Hotel and Dining Rooms in 1888. On the left is the edge of the building on the site of the present garage. Down the hill the scene has not changed except that Cockey's foundry (later the Victoria Baths), seen here beyond the cottages, has recently been demolished.

Christchurch Street East, *c.* 1887. Little of it is now recognizable. The buildings on the right formed part of the Lamb Brewery and were demolished on its closure. On the left, Bath Street Mews, mentioned on the lamp, was run by Frederick Snook until 1887. The new terrace adjoining the Lamb Inn is now on the site. Cockey gas lamps, similar to the one here, were later converted to electricity.

The Wheatsheaf stables, *c.* 1910. This view is very different today, following the demolition of properties along the north side of Palmer Street (see pages 110–11). The courtyard is now bounded by brick buildings. It was in one of these stables that William Langford set up a small press to print medicine-bottle labels, and so founded Butler & Tanner. The chimney belongs to the electricity generating works.

The Old Bath Arms, Palmer Street, *c.* 1900. The steps and the central doorway and window have been replaced but the bracket above is the same. The sign reads 'Bath Arms', and the pub belonged to the Longleat estate until 1899, when it was purchased by Frome United Breweries for £3,000.

Market Place, Frome. — This old town had its origin in a monastery built by St. Aldhelm before 705. The Saxon King, Edred, died at Frome in 955 and was buried at Winchester.

A rare view of this end of the Market Place, *c.* 1910. Jackson's Library was closed by 1918 and the building itself was replaced around 1935 by Montague Burton Ltd, whose name is now hidden above the fascia. The Stroud & Swindon building was erected by the Capital and Counties Bank, later the National Provincial. John Gradidge rebuilt his shop, on the right, in 1899 and sold it in 1923. Notice the lamp standard on a small island at the bottom of the hill, behind the lady.

Market Day, *c.* 1950. This scene is full of activity, with the market stalls, the traffic, and the crowds of people, as typical today as about forty years ago.

Bull's Hotel, Market Place, 1904. The Misses Eliza and Maria Bull opened their Dining and Refreshment Rooms in Bridge Street and in around 1880 took over these newly built premises in the Market Place. Associated with them were livery and posting stables, under job master Thomas Wall, who later moved to Willow Vale. Bull's Hotel continued until November 1914, when the General Post Office moved here from Bath Street.

A procession in the Market Place, *c.* 1914. The ground floor of the shabby-looking building on the corner with Cork Street was first used as a covered market for local butchers, and it had an assembly room above. At the time of this photograph it was probably used for local auctions, judging by the array of sale posters on the walls, which included farms at Stratton and Wanstrow. This procession to St John's is headed by the churchwardens, followed by a thurifer, crucifer, two musicians, choir and, out of sight, the vicar. It was probably part of the St John's Day celebrations at the end of June.

Waterloo House, 18 Stony Street, 12 September 1923. Fear Hill's Stores of Trowbridge have just acquired the drapery business from John Gradidge on his retirement. The posters announce its re-opening on this day so the ladies are expectantly awaiting bargains. The building was erected by Gradidge in 1899.

North Parade, *c.* 1903. The scene has changed little in ninety years except for the traffic, the state of the road surface, and the gas lamp. Above, the view is from just below no. 9, and below, it is level with the present Middleton & Upsall. The terrace on the left (bottom photograph) was built by Charles Rogers, who died in 1823, but its residential use has now virtually gone. Some of the windows have now lost their glazing bars, or have been enlarged when converted to offices.

The Bridge. Moore and Son's, on the left, was a music shop and its fascia still reflects that use. Other shops included Miss Swaine's wool shop, Swaine & Son, tailor and woollen draper, and W. Thick & Son, jeweller. The wall on the other side was removed about thirty years ago to widen the pavement.

The rear of the Bridge, with its higgledy-piggledy arrangement of arches and buildings, would be the delight of any Cornish village. Now the wooden structure has been replaced by a bland modern building and the buildings at each end have also disappeared. The cupola of the Blue House can still be seen peeping over the top.

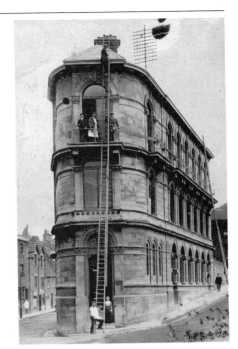

The Literary Institute, 17 July 1913. In conditions which would now give the Health and Safety Executive heart failure, these workmen are repairing The Lit. Its height and position have always presented a problem at the junction of North Parade and Bridge Street. The housing beyond the Black Swan has now gone.

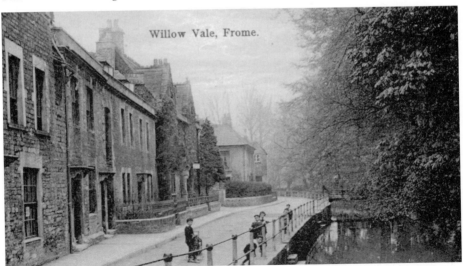

Willow Vale, Frome.

Willow Vale. This view shows the bridge over the river, which was removed when four boys drowned during a flood in 1932. A gate in the railings still marks the spot. The houses on the left have hardly changed but the horse chestnut and copper beech trees on the river bank were felled about thirty years ago as part of a flood prevention scheme, to the detriment of the scene. For many years at Christmas Alan Venn's floodlit cut-outs of a *Snow White* scene adorned the bank until washed away in a flood.

The Town Mill, Willow Vale, 1890. The present river course was then the mill stream, with the river itself meandering nearer Iron Gates and the back of the Blue House. On the left of both photographs is a former dyehouse, with Willow Vale House beyond. The mill was described in 1880 as 'a ruinous building . . . with hatches, washing stand and iron waterwheel' and was run by the Sheppard family, who owned all the land as far as Iron Gates.

Stony Street, *c.* 1907. The first building on the left (no. 10) was then used by Harold Eames, billposter, bookseller and stationer. His wall advertisement reads 'Stationery, Presents, and Fancy Articles'. Oliver's shoe shop (no. 11) is now Harris & Harris; further down are William Joyce's confectioner's and W.H. Smith & Son, before it moved to Bath Street. Beyond the Cockey lamp bracket was Bristol House, run by Mr Bunce, boot and shoe seller. The lower part on the right has little changed, but the buildings which stood on the sites now occupied by Chantings and John Collier are shown. Many fascias and shop fronts have since been 'modernized'.

Catherine Hill, *c.* 1909. This photograph just misses the archway leading to the old Baptist burial ground on the right. On the left W. Earle advertises his picture-frame manufactory. Obviously Mr Dyke attracted interest when preparing to take this photograph.

Catherine Hill. This photograph dates between 1896 and 1906, when Bennett, the seedsman and florist, occupied no. 28 (on the left), as well as the nursery in Nunney Road. The Wheatsheaves, on the left, closed in 1924. The Frome Fish and Game Stores, on the right, was run by Stephen Francis, while below Walter Masterman the butcher advertises Canterbury lamb. At the end of Paul Street Walter Earle was a picture-frame maker. Frisby's, on the left, continued selling shoes until the 1970s; Cottle Bros' confectionery (no. 23) became Catherine Hill Bakery, which was running until recently.

Catherine Hill (not street), *c.* 1914. An iron kerb prevented carts from running away. Cottle's is now Catherine Hill Bakery but the frame for its hanging sign still survives. Dowling & Son, beyond, were tailors and outfitters until 1981 and Percy Coombs, on the right, below Mr Earle, was a hairdresser in Paul Street.

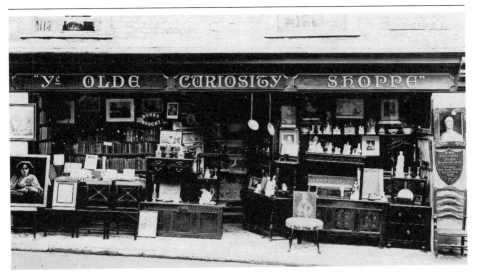

59 Catherine Street, *c.* 1917. These premises on the corner with Whittox Lane are now Bistro Valentinos. The 1912 local directory lists Revd A.O. Shaw as selling furniture and second-hand books here. His display of items is certainly an enticement to look around. The shield on the right advertises 'Antiques, Old China Prints, Second Hand Books'.

51 Catherine Street, October 1921. Mr Knight had extensive premises between the wars at 51–5 Catherine Street, having succeeded S. Knibb & Son, and at 21 Catherine Hill, as carpet warehouseman, house furnisher, draper and milliner. The window display is for a shopping festival and the certificate in the window reads 'Second Prize'. The pilaster on the right, and the shape of the fascia, are still recognizable although the window has been replaced. The premises are now Norton Brokers.

41–2 Catherine Street, *c.* 1905. The covered frontage has now gone but the building above is unchanged, though it is now Sovereign Motorcycles. Dyke's Fancy Bazaar sold a multitude of items, as these two pages of photographs show. Henry Dyke ran the store until his death in 1905. Here his display overflows into the street, all items apparently labelled and orderly. The stonework of the next building up the hill, now Fryer's, has since been rendered. The photograph below is labelled 'The Doll's corner in our new Bazaar'.

New toys at the bazaar: two more views of the arrangement of dolls, train sets, and games which must have made dusting quite an undertaking. By this time the bazaar was run by Henry Dyke's son Frank, who died tragically in 1925, aged forty-six.

Badcox is now much altered. The building just visible on the extreme left, on the corner of Castle Street, is now boarded up owing to planning blight, but there are plans for its restoration. Mr Hodder's pharmacy at the end of Badcox Parade was built by his father in 1890, and is still a chemist's shop; beyond the cart is The Ship. The building on the right, now demolished, was on the site of the present garage; beyond is the garden wall of West Lodge, which is still a doctor's house.

Weymouth Road near the junction with Somerset Road. The park is to the right. The first terrace on the left with bow windows (nos 30–4) was built in about 1887. Beyond, the terrace with a lower roofline (nos 36–52), was built by Thomas Parfitt of Nunney Road in 1871 and named Bath Buildings after Lord Bath, who sold the land for building. Clements Lane was renamed in honour of Lord Bath's heir.

Somerset Road, *c.* 1900. Seward's villa-type housing, dating from the end of the last century, is interesting for the variety of semi-detached properties. The pair on the right, nos 34 and 35, are named St Maur and Rosemorran, and the latter was Christ Church Vicarage from 1968 to 1980. The next pair have round turrets. On the left is the park. The photograph is by H. Dyke.

The Butts, looking back towards the town. The gabled group on the left are now nos 82 and 84, with the site of Cranmore Court beyond. The Seward terrace on the right is now nos 67–73. Imagine the street being traffic-free today.

Keyford, looking towards the Lock's Hill crossroads. The railings have gone, a victim of wartime, while no. 15, on the immediate left, is now a shop with a modern window and concrete front. The building on the right was demolished to widen the entrance to Redland Terrace and The Cooperage.

Keyford from near Lock's Hill, looking away from the crossroads. The shop on the right (no. 33) was Mrs Phyl Crocker's grocery for many years, after the war. Beyond is the unmistakably seventeenth-century cottage, with its gable, and the post office. Beyond is the entrance to Keyford Gardens and the Crown. The terrace on the far left is nos 58–61 (the edge of no. 58 is just visible).

Trinity Street, *c.* 1910. This western part was originally known as Trooper Street, traditionally named after one of Marlborough's troopers, who built the Trooper Inn (no. 11). The building on the left was The Bell and an underground passage ran under the road to the Crown and Sceptre opposite, using a natural fissure in the rock; this enabled beer to be taken from the brewhouse at the rear of the former to the latter. Trinity Church, built in 1838, is at the end of the street.

Milk Street, before 1912. The buildings on the left were all demolished in 1967 but the right-hand side has not really changed, except for the building adjacent to the school, which was replaced in 1912 by classrooms. The square pillared porch dates from 1840 and formed the entrance to the Rechabite Methodist Church, the nucleus of the present school building.

Rodden Road, *c.* 1948. Pre-dating the St John's Road housing estate, this scene has a more rural appearance. Hyde House is on the left, and above it are the roofs of the red-brick terrace. The three-wheeled Morgan belonged to Mr Wheeler, who established the Rodden Road Garage. He lived in one of the old cottages to the right, behind the lamppost.

The Vine Tree Inn, *c.* 1905. It has since been enlarged and there is now a small extension on the left and another which fronts Berkeley Road. However, the inn is still very easily recognizable.

Fromefield looking toward Frome. The building on the left was built in 1835 by the wife of George Sheppard, as a school for the children of his domestic servants and estate workers. On the immediate right is the garden wall of Fromefield House; beyond is 4 Fromefield (see page 106).

Fromefield at the junction with Rodden Road. On the left is the school building mentioned above. The building just visible on the right is now Fromefield post office. Rodden Road now bypasses this junction.

Selwood, 4 Fromefield. These views of the house from the garden and of the drawing room date from its occupation by Thomas Byard Winter Sheppard, between 1895 and his death in 1909.

SECTION NINE

Vanished Frome

Gore Hedge, *c.* 1905. These old cottages stood on the site of the present toilets. One was a butcher's shop, kept for many years by Henry Cray ('Bossie'), who killed the animals on the premises with the words 'Come on, my dear, come and have a bit of Henry's nicey!' In 1905 Lord Bath sold the cottages to the Urban District Council for £175, so that they could be demolished for road widening, and Henry Cray moved briefly to 63 Christchurch Street East.

The Batch, Castle Street. The pavement curved away from Castle Street at the bottom, and the triangle thus formed was known as the Batch, or Coward's Batch. The lower houses of Milk Street can be seen at the end of the path. These were demolished in 1962.

Milk Street, c. 1960. The houses on the left stood opposite Milk Street (now Vallis) School and were demolished in 1962. Behind the building which faces the camera is the Griffin Inn.

Bell Lane ran from Milk Street and turned at right angles to meet Selwood Road. It was named after the Cockey family, who cast church bells here in the eighteenth century. The top view looks towards Milk Street, which is seen at the end, while the photograph below shows the Selwood Printing Works peeping through the gap.

Palmer Street, *c.* 1912. This and the next three views show the north side of Palmer Street before its rebuilding by Frome Co-operative Society. The large building was Frome Mineral Water Co. Ltd, under manager Arthur Wall. The initials over the archway are ROR (Robert O. Reeves), who founded the business. To the left was W. Huxter, dairy and milk seller, listed in a local directory of 1912; his name is on the fascia. On the corner with Stony Street was L.P. Dodge, cabinet maker, upholsterer and ironmonger.

The double-fronted shop of the Frome Co-operative Society opened in 1906. The large posters on the wall advertise Robin Starch and Recketts Blue, both laundry items, and the hanging sign reads 'Agents for Thomson's Dye Works, Perth'. The clock, to the right, indicates Charles Hart the watchmaker, who moved to 21 Bath Street in 1919, and George Smith's hairdresser's window sign lists 'Cigars, Tobacco and Pipes'. Next door was Marchman & Son, the corn dealer, whose managing director was Joseph Moore.

Palmer Street, c. 1912. This interesting house stood on the corner with Bath Street. It appears to date from at least the seventeenth century; note especially the springer arch, and the mullioned windows of the first floor and attics. It was demolished to make way for the present Co-op in 1924. The lines on the stonework of its side show where another house stood before 1810 and the construction of Bath Street.

Bath Street, c. 1912. This is the same house as above. The last owner of the house and shop was Mrs E.J. Foreman, tailor and outfitter. The premises also included the small garden and were sold to the Co-op for £450 in 1919.

Marchant's House, Church Street. This seventeenth-century merchant's house was tragically demolished to make Saxonvale in 1968. It was the home of the Marchant family and the fine first-floor plaster ceiling, dated 1658, contained the initials HM and JM (Henry and Joan Marchant). The ceiling is now preserved at Bradford-on-Avon, as Frome did not want it. The house was often known as the Old Vicarage but was never used as such.

Frome United Brewery, 1958. This was established in 1889 and stood on a site between Broadway, Horton Street and Vallis Way. The site was cleared in 1958 to make way for the Dorset Close housing development. Above, the malthouse is on the left, with the old clothmill building beyond. Below, the malthouse is again on the left, with the main entrance to the yard and main buildings in the foreground.

Wiltshire Buildings, *c.* 1936. This terrace was off Vallis Way, approximately opposite the entrance to Naish's Street. It was demolished in 1936 to make way for Dorset Close.

The Swan Inn, Badcox, stood at the junction of Nunney Road and Broadway and was demolished in 1963. Vallis Way is to the right. The building jutting out at right angles to the road is no. 10, and on the right are nos 39 and 40; the latter is on the corner with Baker Street.

The Lamb Brewery, Gore Hedge. The street on which it stood was spanned by a bridge and this linked the brewery buildings. The brewery closed on 30 September 1957 and was demolished in 1959. The name Gore pre-dates the Monmouth rebellion by many centuries and is Old English for a triangle.

Greenhill Place, c. 1960. A terrace of sixteen cottages stood on the site of the present Gore Hedge flats.

Journal Office, *c.* 1960. The *Somerset and Wilts Journal* was published from 1855 to 1925, when it was absorbed by the *Somerset Standard*. The office stood at the corner of High Street and Catherine Street.

An old toll house. During the eighteenth and early nineteenth centuries Turnpike Trusts were established by Act of Parliament. Many of their milestones and toll houses survive, including most of the former from Frome to Bath, starting in Bridge Street. This toll house and gate stood at the top of North Parade.

Welshmill suspension bridge, 1904. This was erected by James Dredge of Bath in 1842 for a local solicitor, Henry Miller, who lived at Welshmill House. It was to link his garden with land on the other side of the river, and had a span of 51 ft with a deck width of 7 ft 3 in. The bridge was demolished at the start of the last war, presumably for the war effort.

The old band room, Scott Road, *c.* 1960. This was originally a candle factory and was later used by the Frome Town Military Band. It was demolished to make way for the Westway precinct shortly after this photograph was taken. The Literary Institute can just be seen above the wall on the left and an International Stores van is parked on the right. The International then occupied the premises now used by Halfords.

Part of Grove Farm, *c.* 1875. This was the home of the Cabell family in the sixteenth century and was demolished in around 1890. It was sited on part of the present Manor Road industrial estate.

No. 53 Keyford stood at the junction of Keyford and Rossiter's Hill, and was demolished for road widening in 1966.

SECTION TEN
The Villages

Narrow Bridges, Mells, *c.* 1895. The house was a smallholding, but has since been rebuilt following a fire and is now called Bridge Cottage. The bridge has been rebuilt slightly further downstream.

The Bath Arms, Horningsham, *c.* 1907; it is now covered with ivy. The row of trees is part of four rows of three pollarded limes, known as the Twelve Apostles; most are two hundred years old. Below, the inn is on the right with the pollarded limes.

Horningsham, *c.* 1907. Tradition has it that this old Presbyterian chapel was built by Scottish masons who were brought here to build Longleat House, but there is no documentary evidence. If so, it is the oldest Nonconformist chapel in England. The thatch has since been replaced but it is otherwise unchanged.

Longleat: an idyllic scene on the Longleat estate, below Heaven's Gate.

Shearwater, *c.* 1912. The boathouse was destroyed by fire in June 1938, leaving just blackened walls. It was ignited when a spark from a chimney landed on the thatch.

The lake is still a popular beauty spot for an afternoon stroll or for sailing.

Marston Bigot, *c.* 1905. The lodge seen in both views is dated 1834 and has now lost its thatch. The creeper on the tower has also been removed. The wooden gates seen below have also disappeared and a new porch has been added to the front door of the lodge.

Little Green, Mells, *c.* 1900. This scene is almost unrecognizable today. The house on the left has been considerably altered and the adjoining thatched building has gone. The two buildings on the right have been amalgamated and the roof altered; the date 1700 and the initials TP, which were between the windows, have gone. However, the walls of the lane still exist.

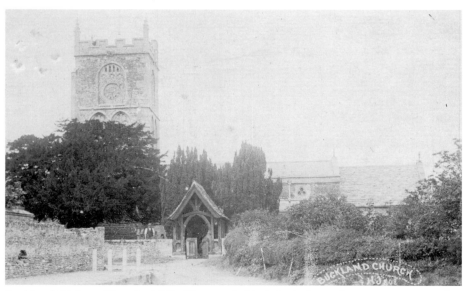

Buckland Dinham Church, 1911. The yew behind the lychgate has now gone, opening up the view to the church, and the pavement has been replaced by the entrance to St Michael's Close. Now there are tidy walls on the right in place of the untidy hedge.

Mells Park. Following the disastrous fire on 11 October 1917, Seward of Frome demolished the remaining parts of the building, as shown here. The park was later rebuilt to the design of Lutyens for Sir Reginald McKenna, cabinet minister and chairman of the Midland Bank.

Nunney Village and Castle, *c.* 1908. The fields in front have now been developed for housing and the castle has lost its creeper.

Nunney Rectory and Market Place, *c.* 1950. The building in the centre right is still much the same, except that the top left window has lost its glazing bars and a doorway has been added. The building adjoining it has lost its creeper and now has an additional floor. The Old Rectory, at the end of the road, is now a residential home for the elderly.

Lullington, *c.* 1905. Above, the lychgate is the same but the view of the church has been improved. Below, the cottages on the left were replaced in 1927 by Mr Duckworth. The village pump is hidden by the small tree in front of the cottage on the far right.

Orchardleigh, *c.* 1905. The island church in Orchardleigh Park is the burial place of Sir Henry Newbolt, famous for 'Drake's Drum' and other poems. Sir Henry married a Duckworth. The future of the park and the house is still in doubt.

Rodden church, 1905. Little has changed since this photograph was taken, except that the lighting is now electric and the floor has been carpeted. The church was built in 1640 to serve a village now mostly gone.